Too Many Wife-in-Laws

MISS GOLDIE

PAGE PUBLISHING, INC.
New York, NY

First originally published by Page Publishing, Inc. 2018

ISBN 978-1-64138-745-3 (Paperback)
ISBN 978-1-64138-746-0 (Digital)

Printed in the United States of America

*H*ere I go again, Miss Goldie back on the track. I'm back running the Gary Motel on Stewart Avenue. I haven't heard from Slim anymore after we went our separate ways. Somebody said he was on the run from the Feds and that he was on FBI's ten most wanted. They said in the newspaper that he's the East Coast supplier. I just kept thinking, Pimp God had my back because of all the dope and money me and my family had to bag up and count. Then I find out he's married. I had to get the fuck on. Then he gets mad because, when I left him, fifty thousand went with me. The first thing I did was buy me a Jaguar.

I'm sitting here bagging up the last dope I have. Slim was the only drug dealer I knew with weight. I can't call him. He's on the run, plus I was scared to call his number. I remember the pimp slash drug dealer that my cousin knew. His name was Drake, and he had given me his number when he came on Stewart Avenue.

I really didn't pay him any attention when he kept saying, "I finally meet the famous Miss Goldie that everybody talks about."

When I turned around and saw who was talking to me, I kind of blushed a little. He was dark-skinned with diamonds in his mouth and had his hair permed with finger waves. His hair was long, and when he opened his mouth, he sounded like Michael Jackson. Now that freaked me out. Hell, I just wanted to know if he could sing after I heard him speak.

My cousin laughed at me all night because I kept saying can he sing like Mike.

She kept laughing and said, "No, girl." Then she said, "Hell I don't know if he can sing at all. I just know he got good dope, the best in the club, but not better than what you're used to."

I had to pick up the keys of dope when it got to the pickup spot. Then I and my brother-in-law had to break the block up and put it in ounces. That shit took all night, so we had to get a hotel room because I stopped bringing all that shit to my house. Only thing I would take back home is five ounces to bag up. The rest stayed in the hotel ceiling.

I got my own trap now, plus I know what kind of dope I want. Slim taught me well. I'm running the motel for Hilda. I hit me a sting every now and then. I'm about to leave them tricks alone and just work on my dope trap I got on Auburn Avenue. I already got half the pimps and hoes getting their dope from me. It's crazy, because I used to stand on this same corner, being pimped to death by Saint James, who turned me out. Now he's my baby daddy and one of my customers, who buy dope from one of my boys. Hell, I got a couple of soldiers working for me on Auburn Avenue, and they're loyal. One of my workers got his own apartment, so we trap out of it. Then I got my regular customers who buy dope out by my house. I was taking good care of my family, but I picked up this bad habit.

I started putting powder in a cigarette. Big mistake. It started clouding my brain. I was sitting at home and the phone rang. I needed some weight but not that big of a weight. I had been putting powder in my cigarette so much that I didn't realize I was fucking up my profit. Now my phone was ringing, and on the other end was a nigger with plenty dope calling me. I said, "Damn, I was just thinking about this boy."

He said, "This is Drake."

I said, "Drake."

He said, "I'm the one who came down on Stewart Avenue, and your cousin was with you. She dances at the strip club that I be at."

I said, "Oh yell, you the one who got some girls working at the strip club."

I remember what my cousin said about his hoes. All of them was on crack, and he supplied his hoes. He was a kingpin, she said.

I said to him, "I need some work for my trap."

He said, "You got a trap."

I said, "Yell, don't you?" He asked me where I lived at. I told him in the Deck. That stands for Decatur."

He said to me, "I stay in the Deck."

Drake came over, and I was kind of excited because I wanted to hear him talk like Michael Jackson again. I had satin sheets on the bed and curtains to match. I had all colors of satin sheets and curtains to match. When he walked in, he asked who owned the Jaguar outside. I told him it was mine. He said he liked it, and I told him I didn't have a license and I had to get the steering wheel fixed again after I thought they fixed it before I left the lot. They didn't know what they were doing, and the steering wheel cracked again.

When Drake walked into my room, he said, "Damn, girl. I'm scared to sit on your bed. It's so pretty."

I told him, "It's okay, you can sit. It's just a bed."

I told Drake what I needed and gave him some money for an ounce. He was smelling so good, so I asked him if he wanted to watch at a movie. He said sure. I popped a movie in the VCR. He kicked his shoes off and scooped back on the pillows. I had just gotten out the shower before he got there, so I just had on a robe with nothing underneath.

I had put on a little perfume, and I can tell he liked it because when I sat beside him on the bed, he put his nose up against my neck and said in a sexy voice, "Damn, girl, you smell good as hell."

I found myself kissing this man, and my body was on fire like nothing I had ever experienced before. I found myself licking this man like I was a dog. I started sucking his dick like I was trying to get to the bubble gum on a lollipop. He moaned and moaned until he couldn't moan anymore. Then he put his hands over his mouth because I wasn't releasing this dick. It was too good to take out my mouth, plus it smelled so good. The veins in his dick was pounding, so I released his dick because I knew he couldn't handle a veteran hoe like me. He laid me on my back and opened my legs wide. My pussy was already wet as hell from sucking his dick. He put his hands under my butt and ate my pussy until I screamed in my pillow like I had never been scared before. He didn't let go after that first nut I caught. He stuck his big-ass dick in my pussy so I can nut on it instead of nutting in his mouth.

Then he took his dick out when my pussy stopped jerking and started to suck it again. When I was about to cum a second time, he turned me on my stomach and stuck his dick all the way in and rotated his body. While I was cuming, so was he. We came together, and we both were trying hard not to scream out, so we buried our faces in the pillows.

And before we fell asleep, he said, "I stayed on that pussy because it tastes so damn good." I smiled and fell asleep in his arms.

While we were sleeping, his two beepers had been blowing up and so was mine. We got up and showered. I put on something sexy to wear for today, and he asked me if I would ride with him today and put work off for him. Before I knew it, I was calling my trap and Hilda at the motel. I told them I was not working today and I would see them later through the week. We left my house and got something to eat. While we were eating, he was telling me about the three strippers he had living with him.

While he was talking, the only thing I was thinking was, *What the hell am I doing with this pimp slash drug dealer?*

We got to Drake's house, and his girls looked pissed at him, but they didn't say anything to him. He called all the girls in the living room and introduced me to them. I didn't know that so many strippers had heard of me. I never really thought much of strippers because they had to dance and bend over all night just to make two hundred dollars, then you got to pay bar fee. Hell, at the end of the night, you ain't hardly got shit to take home.

The girls were trying to talk at one time, and he said, "Damn, I guess you all heard of Miss Goldie too." The girls were saying, "Miss Goldie, I heard you whip bitch's ass on the track and you got your own motel."

I said, "No, I don't own no motel."

Now that's a lie. I run one, but my friend owned it. She was from Germany.

The girls were on crack, and one of them was still in high school. She was so bad she had been in the twelve grade for three years. She was working for Drake at the strip club. She was a light-skinned, small, petite girl who was twenty-one but refused to drop out of school. I respected her for still being in school even though she was the oldest one in school. His other girl was mixed with black and white blood. She had a beautiful hair and she was pretty, but some of her teeth looked rotten, and she twitched her mouth a little, and she wasn't from Atlanta. The other girl wasn't from Atlanta either. Her body lookedfunny, and her stomach looked like a small knot in it like a high hornya. I didn't understand why he had her even though she was sweet. Sweet doesn't pay no damn bills. I said to myself, *This nigger is running rest haven for hoes, or should I say strippers.* Hell, I don't know. I just know I want some more of that dick of his, and I'll do anything for him to give it to me.

Drake took me to a motel when we left his house. I didn't understand why we went to a motel instead of my house. I found out when he started sucking and fucking me like it was the end of the world. I screamed out in ecstasy and no pillow could hold back my scream. The manager knocked on the door and asked if everything was all right. We answered the door laughing.

The manager said, "Hold it down."

We left and went and got dinner. He wasn't even thinking about them hoes. We just left. He only concentrated on me that whole day. He answered his beepers when his boys call from the dope trap, and he told them where to take his money. It reminded me of Slim, and then I knew that I wasn't over him. I still was in love with him no matter what. I knew this man couldn't take his place no matter how much dope he might have.

I still haven't told Drake I would be with him. He has come over every night for a week. I haven't given him any choosing money, and he ain't asking for any. I came to the conclusion that this is no pimp, simply yell, but not a pimp bone in this nigger body. I was still putting dope in those damn cigarettes, and my profit was disappearing. I had become my best customer, so I knew what I had to do.

Drake came over that night, and I had fixed dinner for us.

After dinner, we made passionate love, and I told him, "I want to be with you. I choose you."

He looked at me when I handed him five hundred.

He said, "What this for?"

That night, he became a pimp because I told him what kind of hoe I was and what I expected out of them as wives-in-law.

I told him I know they smoke crack and sell dope out the strip club. I ask him how that worked. I told him if those hoes are smoking crack, then they are their best customer. They were being the dope. Then I asked him how much stripper money they are getting.

Before he could answer, I said, "Don't tell me."

It was a slow night every night, but the dope money she brought in was all there.

I said, "Boy, I'm about to save you." Little did I know that he was a devil out to get me.

Drake asked me if I would move in with him and them hoes. I moved in the next day. The young girl that was in school was talking about leaving because he haven't been home, and they knew he was with me. He had a bottom hoe, which was the mix girl from up north. She seems to not care if he come home or not as long as she got her dope for work. The boys were dropping that off to them before they get to the strip club, she and his other girl. They told him, when we got there, that the young girl have not been going to work or school since he'd been gone. His bottom hoe was cleaning out drawers for me to put some of my clothes in.

He told her, "I would be sleeping with them."

Drake's other two girls had their own rooms. Drake went inside the young girl's room, and when he came out, he told us to take her to school. She came out the room, and it looked like she had been crying. We took her to school, me and my wife-in-law. When we got back, there were some bags by the front door. All my things were in the bedroom that the young girl was in. Both of my wives-in-law asked me to ask Drake what was going on. They acted like they were scared to say something.

I said, "Daddy, what's going on?"

They didn't call him daddy and didn't know he loved when you call him that, especially when we're in bed. They didn't have a clue who this man really is as long as they get their dope.

He said, "When you'll pick that bitch up from school, take these clothes with you all, and tell that bitch it's over. Tell her I'll call her ass later. Take her to her mommy's house."

When she called and said that school was out, we left to pick her up. When she got in the car, my wives-in-law told her what he said. She went ham, and we drove fast to get this bitch out of the car.

She told me, "All he does is run around and fuck anything that moves. You will see for yourself, Miss Goldie. When he brings all them different hoes home, you going to see."

I said to myself, *As long as them bitches got choosing money, I wouldn't give a fuck how many hoes come home.*

We drop the young girl home and stopped and got something to eat. When we got back, I checked on my girls. I was going to have to go from Drake's house to my house because I had my two daughters. The next day, it was about twelve noon, Drake had already said he didn't want me on the track all night. He said all his ladies must be in the house before three in the morning or after the strip club closed. I knew Hilda would be working at the motel. I didn't want her to know I had chosen again. I told Drake to park his car in the back. He said, "How long are you going to be?"

I said, "Give me ten minutes."

A car pulled up and before I knew it, I was getting back in the car with Drake, telling him let's go. He said if it slowed, I can bring you back. Before he could finish talking, I was pulling out a big-ass knot. He said, "It's true what they said about you. You the baddest thief I have ever seen."

I said, "Here, daddy, it's seventeen hundred."

He said, "Dollars?"

I said, "Yes."

He said, "I got me something special."

When we got home, he called both of my wives-in-law and bragged about how much money I just made in ten minutes. When he pulled the money out, you would've thought it was Christmas the way he was acting. I knew I would not be here long.

A year passed by, and I was getting so much money. Drake told me that he caught this hoe, that had taken a quarter key from this dope boy.

He said, "The hoe is on her way over here now."

I said, "If this bitch is setting us up, I'm going to whip her ass."

My wives-in-law said, "You know she's not playing."

I had touched that bottom bitch of his up the second week I moved in with him. I waited until he left the house. I told that bitch to talk that smart ass shit now. Soon, as she opened her mouth, I punched that bitch in her mouth. She ran and locked herself in the bathroom until Drake got there.

He said, "I was wondering how long was it going to take before you beat her ass."

They saw that he had a real hoe in his stable, and they were scared as hell.

I was in my new bedroom. I had got so much money he was buying big weight now. We had moved to a bigger condo, and everything was new. He and his bottom bitch still had the same room, but he slept with me. We fucked every night, and he didn't care who heard us. We fucked on the bathroom floor if he saw me in the bathroom. Whatever part of the house he saw me at, we always ended up fucking. My wives-in-law started taking walks when they heard us.

I told him, "You know their feelings are hurt."

He said, "I don't care. They need to start getting money like you instead of buying dope for themselves, like I'm stupid. That's why I don't fuck them hoes unless you say they can join us."

Sometimes I would let my other wife-in-law join us and give me some head. He liked that.

Drake let his girls put crack and weed in cigarettes. I didn't play that shit, so I only put powder in cigarettes. He was always asking me why I don't put crack in the cigarettes. I told him about my baby daddy free basting with a pipe and golden grain.

I told him, "I don't care how you do crack. It still takes your ass out of the game."

He said if he ever finds out his girls were smoking crack on a pipe or a can, they ass out of here. I asked him if people smoke crack out of a can. He said a lot of them hoes in the strip club do.

I was getting out of the tub and Drake came in, saying he needed to make an announcement. Before I can finish drying off, he had me doggy style. We were all over the bathroom floor. The trash can turned over, and a can hit the floor. We stopped and started putting the trash back in the can.

I picked up the can and said, "I guess they didn't have an ashtray. That's why they used the can."

Drake grabbed the can out of my hand and looked at how it was bent. He said hell no, then all hell broke loose. I said to myself why I had to be the one to find the can.

Drake said family meeting, and we all piled up in the living room. He told one of the girls to go get pens and paper. She asked how many pens; he said two.

When she came back, he said, "Hand one of the pens to your wife-in-law." She tried to hand me a pen, and he said, "No, bitch, your other wife-in-law." Then he told her to hand her some paper to write with, and she did.

Drake said, "I want you'll two hoes to write a thousand times, 'I must try to get as much money as Miss Goldie.'"

They didn't ask any question; they just started writing.

Drake said, "When you'll get finish, I got something good for you girls."

They smiled a little and started joking about running out of paper. I guess he was going to give them some crack to smoke. I was wondering why he haven't mentioned the can we found in the bathroom.

The doorbell rang, and Drake said, "You'll hoes take a break from writing and start cooking."

I was in my bedroom when I heard someone say, "Miss Goldie, come here."

Drake had opened the door, and this chick came in with a book bag. Drake got the bag from the broad and went in the back. I followed him in the back while my wives-in-law kept cooking.

Drake looked in the bag, and it was four ounces in there.

I looked at him and said, "I guess this is her choosing money."

He said, "I guess it is." We started to laugh until we heard one of the girls say, "You'll better come get this bitch." We headed to the kitchen, and one of my wives was in the girl's face. Drake got in between them.

I asked what was going on, and the chick responded, "Don't worry about what the fuck was going on. Drake, I didn't know you had so many hoes. I'm not with that shit. You can give me my man shit back."

Before I knew it, I was beating this bitch all the way out of the door.

Drake went outside and pulled me off her ass. She asked for her keys, and Drake handed them to her and told her she better run and not look back before he let me go on her ass again.

When I went inside, my wives were laughing and saying, "I knew you were going to get her."

When they finished cooking, they had to start back writing what Drake told them to write. They wanted that surprise he had for them when they finish. Drake didn't smoke or drink, and he never did drugs because he grew up around it in the projects.

His mom still stayed in the projects, but he had gotten her a store, where she sold antiques and different kinds of pictures that go on the wall. She was a very nice lady, and she knew what her son did. He had her counting all his money and putting it up. We never saw where the money goes, and I didn't like that at all. He said he was getting her out of the project and buying her a house.

Drake had bought a long black table, and it was made of marble and had ten chair to go with it—four on each side and the two chairs that sat at the head of the table. He sat a triple bean scale on the table and told me to come to him. He laid a key of dope on the table and told me to bag it in ounces. He said I got an announcement to make. "You'll want be going to work anymore, no track and no strip club. That's over. For now on, you'll job is to cook and bag up all the dope. Miss Goldie is the only one that can touch the dope. You'll hoes are going to open all the bags up."

When those hoes finished writing, Drake said, "Which one of you hoes smoking dope out of a can, like a real crackhead?"

Both of them said, "Not me."

He called his bottom hoe in the room. Next thing I heard was screaming and pleading for him to stop beating her. He beat her for an hour with a belt. Then when he got tired of beating her with the beat, he beat her with his fist. Then he called my other wife in her room and beat her until he fractured her ribs. That's the only reason why he stopped beating her—she had passed out.

He gave them hoes dope to smoke that night because I told him that's the least you can do after the ass whipping they just got. He told me about his brother was a dope fiend. He said he had been trying for years to get him off. The only thing I kept thinking was, there was no damn excuse for you to beat them girls like that. That's when I lost respect for him. I said to myself, if he beat them like that, what will he do to me if I leave him?

I was weighing up the keys and passing it down to my wives to put in bags. There was a knock on the door and they said it was US marshals. We asked them who they were looking for, and they said one of my wives' name. With all that dope on the table and on the stove cooking, I told her to get her jacket and run in the back, and I got her some money and pushed that bitch out the door. I called Drake and told him to come home. Lately, he been disappearing on me and not answering the phone for a long time.

He had bought a Mercedes, and we had phones in our cars. I had my Jaguar fixed, so I and my wives-in-law would go riding when we finished bagging up the dope for the traps. One of my wives had a sugar daddy that she had been dating since the strip club. He was in a wheelchair and was from Miami. He sold dope and would give her dope and money. We never told on her because we used to pick her back up before we head home.

One of the girls said, "Goldie, you know, they were talking about Drake don't got some square bitch pregnant. That's what the streets are saying."

I said, "Oh hell, is that why he been disappearing on us?"

I guess he doesn't know me at all, but he will.

When Drake got home, I told him that the US marshals took his bottom hoe. They said something about her being wanted in Jamaica. He knew what I was talking about and called an attorney. She stayed in jail for three months, and we continued cooking and bagging up dope. My wife-in-law was in the federal jail out there in Douglas County until they see if the United States have a treaty with Jamaica. If they don't, then she will be released. Drake said she got caught bringing dope through the airport before he met her. He said she was with this big-time player up north. He said that's why she ended up here in Atlanta. I said that bitch had been running, and she liked to get us fucked up too. He said, "We are not cooking or bagging up here at the house anymore. I got another apartment for us. Let's go, pick up the keys, and put a little furniture in it."

We left to go see the new apartment, me and my wife-in-law. He never slept with her again after he found that can she had been smoking on. That had been over a year, and he never mentioned it again. He said she was the only one who knew how to cook the dope good, and boy, she had to cook a lot, and I had to stand over her and watch her like a hawk. When the dope is finished, then I take over. I let her have whatever shake's left, and that was a lot, but I didn't let Drake know that. If my suspicion is right, she wanted to be smoking for a while because he might just kill her and I might have to save her.

My wife had got out of jail, and Drake was still not coming home. He said to tell my wife that she needed to bag dope only. She couldn't touch anything but what he gives her to bag up. This was his bottom bitch he treated that way, and I didn't like that. I knew a kingpin friend of mine that been buying weight from me. He was asking about her. He had it bad for her, I could tell, plus when she was locked up, he sent her plenty of money and pretended it came from me. It was time for her to meet him. I was thinking, I had been going back and forth from my house to Drake's house. Since the keys were dropped off to me, I had to break them down, the same way I did when I was with Slim. I took my shit off the top until I had my own key of dope. I took my dope to my house and had my sister and brother running my trap. In my bedroom at Drake's house, I had an ounce of dope in nearly every damn shoe. He never had to come home, I was thinking. Why I was home, I get this phone call, and I couldn't say a word for the first time.

On the other end of the phone was Slim. A part of me was glad to hear from him, another part of me was wondering, *Why are you calling me? Aren't you running from the Feds?* I know I will always appreciate him from taking me off the track. I always called him my prince, and I had never gotten over him even when he told me he was married after being with me almost two years. I felt sorry for his wife because she had gotten on crack, bagging up all his dope, and because she was married to a kingpin, she was getting locked up with him. Alone with the rest of his family. Why the hell was he calling me for?

He said, "What's up?"

I said, "What's up with you?"

He said, "I want to see you. I missed you."

Before I knew it, I was meeting him in our old trap. When I got there, his boys were out there trapping. It was like business as usual. I thought he was running, and I wasn't going to ask. When I pulled up, they didn't know who was in that cocaine-white Jaguar with white interior. I stepped out of the car, and the boys looked like they have fainted. They haven't seen me since I took that fifty thousand that we had made that day.

They kept saying, "Hell no, what's up, Miss Goldie? I like that Jaguar, that motherfucker is the baddest thing I've seen yet."

Slim came from around the building, and he looked fine as hell. Lord knows I need some dick bad. I haven't fucked Drake in six months, I know. Drake had this other kingpin friend that had a dope trap downtown. He would come every other day to buy big weight from me. He been trying to hit on me every time he came over, but I never gave him the time of day. I always thought they were setting me up. He asked me if we could cook his dope up, and he would pay us. Drake said that will be okay for us to make extra money. What he didn't know was this man wanted me bad, and he said he won't stop until I'm his. Little that he knew I didn't want anyone but Slim.

Slim jumped in the car, and we drove up the street from the trap, and we parked on a small deserted street. We didn't say a word. We were taking our clothes off so fast we forgot where we were. Before you know it, we were in the backseat, fucking like it was the end of the world. We were there for an hour, and I had caught three nuts to his two. The car was smelling like sex, and we lay back and didn't speak. Finally, I told him I had to get back. He said he had to get back as well. He said he was sorry he didn't do right by me. I planned on keep seeing him until I can't anymore, I told myself.

I didn't ask Slim about his wife or the problems he was facing. I just wanted to be with him no matter what. We sneaked around for a while until, one day, my Jag was in the shop. I took one of the other cars because Drake said he didn't know when it will be ready. Drake had caught two other girls, and they worked at the strip club in the west end. Slim had been calling me, so I was going to kill two birds with one stone. Drop the girls off and go fuck Slim right quick. I had just dropped the girls off and was headed to Slim's trap. I didn't see him where I picked him up the last time. I drove around for a little while. Then out of nowhere, a car hit me, and I'm in Slim's trap that Drake knows about. I'm fucked. The guy that hit me was in his grandmother car, and he wasn't supposed to be in that neighborhood and neither did I. We came up with a solution. Since the expressway was a block away, we both drove up there and acted like that's where the accident happened by the expressway. It worked like a charm, or so I thought.

The girl they said he had gotten pregnant was the sister of one of my old friends from the Purple Onion strip club. We were going to be roommates until my brother had me fired and locked up for being underage and for using his baby mommy ID. I still knew the club number, so I told one of the girls to tell her to call me, and she did.

I said, "What's up, lady?"

She said, "Girl, you know my little sister."

I remember her little sister when we used to hang together on our day off, plus she had been trying to get me to get with her man after we didn't live together like we wanted to. That girl had the hairiest pussy you ever wanted to see. It looked like a forest between her legs. She was the hairy dancer, they called her. Only thing was sticking out was her spur tongue. Which was fat as hell. She made a lot of money every night.

She said, "I been trying to get in touch with you for the longest. Where should I start? First, my little sister in the twelfth grade was pregnant by Drake. Then she had a miscarriage. Drake doesn't want nothing to do with her now. I see him coming in the club, picking up this girl that they say is your cousin."

I said, "My cousin?"

She called out her name, and I said, "Oh yell."

I went and told my wives-in-law what our man been up to.

They looked at me and said, "We already knew. You had been gone and been too busy."

I said, "What about my cousin? Have you heard anything about him and her?"

My wife said, "Girl, you go to bed early, we don't. We just pretend we are asleep because of all the dope you give us after we finish cooking and bagging. He can't know that we have that much to smoke, so we pretend we are asleep when he comes home. One night, he brought your cousin home. You were sleep. He fucked her on the living room floor and gave her some dope."

I said, "Are y'all sure, because I had been bringing her ass over here, plus get her ass high and give her crack to take with her so she can have something for later?"

I gave that bitch money when she didn't make any on Stewart Avenue. I even forgave that bitch when she stole that dope out of my room when I was in the shower. I told my man not to hurt her when he found her. I told him to let her go. That dirty bitch, she was going to pay for that shit. I told my wives-in-law.

His bottom hoe was tired of the disrespect. She started kicking it with a friend of mine that sold weight. He didn't care about her smoking crack in the cigarettes because he did the same thing. Drake never knew. My other wife-in-law was pregnant by the trick in the wheelchair that she had been fucking because Drake stopped fucking both of my wives when he found that can in the garbage that they had been smoking crack on. He didn't know she was pregnant because she wore baggy clothes, and it look like she was just gaining weight. The other two hoes had last two days. When they left, I kept telling Drake I believe they were sent here to case the place out. They were sent by someone.

Drake said, "You're paranoid. You need to stop smoking powder in those cigarettes because you'll be tripping with everyone. I know them girls from the club. They probably got scared of you because you run all hoes off that I bring home. The other girls don't say a word, only you, then they're gone."

I wanted to tell him, "That's because you're running a rest haven for hoes. Boy, you don't have a damn pimp bone in your damn body."

I called my cousin and asked her what was up.

She said, "I know you're going to be mad at me. I need to tell you about your man."

I told her, "I already heard how you fucked him while I was sleep one night. Is that how you're doing it? Well, I'm going to tell you like this, I don't give a fuck. I've been fucking Slim anyway, and I'm going to see him every chance I get over there in his trap. That's where Drake's car got hit at in Slim trap."

What I didn't know was that Drake had to use the phone, and I didn't hear him pick up the phone and heard my whole conversation.

I said to myself, "All hell is about to break loose."

I hung up with my cousin and went to take a bath. When I got out the tub, Drake was in my room, waiting for me.

He said, "Oh, you going to see your ex now?"

That's the only thing I could remember because he beat me unconscious. When I woke up, it was three in the morning, and my wives-in-law were lying beside me in my room. They said they had been putting cold ice on my face all night. I got up and looked at my face. I couldn't recognize myself in the mirror. I knew this was over, and I would be leaving soon before I catch a murder case.

It had been three weeks since I talked to Slim. His wife got my number out of his beeper and threatened to tell Drake if I call there again. She said she knew all about the hoe he got. She said they were expecting a baby and to never call him again. I had been fucking Drake lately because he felt bad about what he did. He kept saying he didn't fuck my cousin, that was a lie. He didn't know my wives heard them.

He's such a liar, I thought to myself. Lately he been staying at home, and I was wondering what he was up to.

I soon found out when he called a family meeting. Everybody piled up in the living room.

Drake said, "I heard one of you hoes is pregnant by one of those Miami boys. The one in the wheelchair."

No one said a word.

Then he said, "I also heard one of you hoes fucking around with one of my partners. You'll go to your rooms, you'll discuss me."

Everybody went to their rooms, and all hell broke loose.

I heard my wife, the one that's pregnant, screaming. I came out of my room and burst into hers. Drake was beating her all in her face. He ripped her clothes off, and when he did, my other wife had come in the room to help me get him off her. We all stood there looking at how big she really was. Drake told her to call her family out of state and tell them you're coming home. We helped her pack all her belonging, then he called his bottom hoe in the room. He couldn't get my wife that was pregnant like he wanted, so he took it out on his bottom bitch because he beat the truth out of her, and she confessed to fucking his friend and said it was because he disrespected her so many times. She never mentioned I'm the one that set her up with the dude.

My wife couldn't get out of bed; she had to go to the hospital. I think her ribs were cracked. Drake had really done it this time. I took her to the hospital, and they said her ribs were bruise from the fall down the steps. That's what she told them, that she fell down the steps. When we got to the hospital, her friend was there. I told him to get the fuck out because Drake knew. He said Drake called him and asked him if he was fucking his wife. He told him no.

He said that Drake said, "Why is it that my boys saw you'll going in a room and staying for hours? They said you'll always going to that motel. They're just telling me now that you been knocking my girl off."

I told him that was a lie. He told me to get my shit from some-body else's, and he better not ever see me at his house. That was what he said, but I didn't care. I came to check on her. She had called him.

We headed home, and I didn't ask her what they talked about. When we got there, Drake had my wife that was pregnant cooking something to eat. He sat there watching her cook. He said, "This bitch might poison me. That's why I'm watching her cook my food." My wife could cook, and she always had me help her. Drake said, "We are going on vacation to Miami before my wife leave for up north." He gave her a couple thousand dollars to take with her when she leaves for up north. All the money he had in the safe, in my bed-room, he only gave her that measly two thousand dollars. She had been with him for ten years and had been cooking his dope for him since she been with him, plus danced at the club. His bottom hoe had been with him for twelve years, and look at how he treated them since his money had got huge. His mother had the big money in the bank. She had to wash the money through the antique shop.

I didn't understand the reason we were going to Miam, but I was happy because I had never been there before. I've been to Baltimore because my sister lived there. When I was younger, I used to spend my summer there. I would come back to Atlanta, talking like a white girl. My brother would get mad and punch me and start screaming, "Talk right, talk right." My mom would laugh so hard at him. I didn't think it was funny; those punches hurt.

We all packed for Miami, and we were excited to be there. I wanted to go on Byscain Boulevard. They say that's where all the pimps and hoes hang out.

Drake said, "You are a real hoe, aren't you?"

I said, "I'm sure is."

My wives started laughing and saying, "No work, Goldie, okay?"

I said, "Okay, let's have some fun."

Drake had to meet his connect so he can pay cheaper for the weight. All of us had lump sums of money on us. I guess I know now why Drake brought us down here—to carry the money, not for no damn vacation. I was wondering how he was going to get the dope back when someone knocked on the door.

It was Drake's boys, and they had driven down here before we got here. They were in a room across from ours. When they came in they had a duffel bag. In the bag, there were guns. Drake reached in the bag and got his three 57s that I thought was at home. He handed me my .38 that I thought was at home.

Then both of my wives said, "Don't tell me you got our guns with you too?"

Drake bought all of us guns at the pawnshop. Him and his mother didn't want any hot guns in the house, and since Drake had never been in trouble before, he was able to buy anything he wanted. He always took us to the shooting range; sometimes we compete with one another. All of us knew how to change the clip fast as well.

I said, "What the hell's going on, Drake?"

He said, "The boys are carrying a hundred thousand dollars. We got fifty thousand dollars. We're about to buy these keys. I don't want to get robbed, do you? Plus, you'll know how to shoot."

Then he passed out the bulletproof vest, and I liked to have fainted.

I said to my wives, "Put the bathing suits up."

This vacation has ended before it started.

There was a pool downstairs, and it was inside of the building. It had glass around; it was in a private room to itself. The meeting would take place down here. We all headed to the pool with our clothes on. We had our guns wrapped in our towels. We had the duffel bag of money with us, and one of the boys was carrying it. Each one of us had a guy on our arm, like we were together. I walked with Drake and my wives were walking with the other guys and were holding their hands like couples. Everybody went their separate ways when we left the room. One by one, we stoodup at the pool, and Drake was with the connect. I was about to faint with that bulletproof vest on. I kept wondering, where the hell did they got those from? But I didn't want to know, so I didn't ask. I knew I was getting the fuck on, and it was just a matter of time when I left.

Everything went good, and we were headed back home from the airport. The boys had the dope with them, and it would be a little while before they reach Georgia. We turned in our subdivision and parked the car in the driveway. For some reason, something didn't feel right. I didn't say anything because everybody was talking about being glad to be home. When we walked in, we already knew somebody had been in our house. Drake ran to the back where the safe was. We had taken most of the money with us, except for about twenty thousand. When Drake looked in the safe, both his jewelry and mine were gone. We about to have a big family meeting, and I hoped I'd be gone.

I haven't talked to Slim in a month, and I was wondering where he was, and I was in a deep thought when Drake started kissing on my neck, horse playing. He used to always say I act like a tomboy. I had some wrestling moves and I used to put him in a headlock and he couldn't get out. He was trying to take our mind off the burglary. Everybody started laughing when we were wrestling until he put me in a figure 4. That's when somebody put their legs around your waist and squeeze. I screamed so loud that everybody stopped laughing and he let me go. I fainted, and they rushed me to the hospital.

We went straight to the emergency room. That's the last thing I remember before I woke up three days later. The doctor came in and said I had a miscarriage. He said I had twins and that one of the babies went in my tube. I called Slim from the hospital phone. I knew his wife didn't know that number. He answered, and I told him what happened and that I was going home to my house when I leave the hospital. It would be over ten years before I see Slim again.

Drake came to the hospital, and the doctor told him what happened. He thought it was his babies, and he was upset. When we got home, everybody was over there, discussing about what they were going to do about the people who broke in the house. Drake had moved some girl he grew up with in the house. She was on crack, and from what the streets were saying, he'd been fucking her and been taking her shopping. I didn't give a fuck because I had money and dope at home in my trap. I called Drake in the room and told him I was leaving. He asked me if I was sure I wanted to leave because he just bought us a big house. I told him he just bought him a big house. I already have a house.

I packed up my Jaguar with my clothes, TV, and VCR and told Drake to give me two thousand dollars and some dope. He did, and I told everybody before I left, especially the new girl, that he's running a rest haven for hoes.

I told her, "Look, little bitch, I hope you get everything you deserve because Lord knows you ain't paid a dime to be here. Now say something smart."

Drake said, "Come on, Goldie, you said you are leaving, so that's on you." A horn blew outside, and it was my wife-in-law, the one that got pregnant, and her family; she was leaving too.

Drake looked at his bottom hoe and asked her was she next. She said, "I'm not going anywhere." I stayed for a while, helping my wife get her stuff. Her family didn't want to step foot in the house, so I helped her get her stuff. We were going over the condo, making sure we had all our belonging, when Drake got a phone call and left with two guns.

He said, "Could you at least stay until I come back? I'll have my mom go to the bank and get you a little more money, okay? I don't trust these hoes, in case something happens to me."

I asked him what he was talking about.

He said, "I'm about to go get those boys who broke into our house."

I said, "Drake, please let it go." I wouldn't want anything to happen to him, so I stayed until he got back, if he got back.

When Drake got back, he didn't say a word. I asked him if he was okay, and he said no. I left, going home. The next day, Drake called me and told me he had done something to some guys who stayed around by where I lived.

I told him, "Let me see. What's going on? I'll call him back."

I called one of my nephews, and he said that them boys around the corner were the ones who broke in his house, and one of his boys set it up.

I said, "Oh yell."

I called Drake and told him that one of his boys set him up. He asked me which one. I told him I didn't know, but I will find out. After doing my investigation, I found out it wasn't one of the boys. It was that hoe he told where we lived at whom he got that dope from. She had ripped off this drug dealer and thought she was going to be with Drake by herself. He forgot to mention to that dumb bitch he had three hoes living with him. When she realized that she asked him for the dope back and started cursing his ass out.

When he said, "You'll get this bitch out my house," that's all I had to hear. I dragged that bitch and whipped her like she was my child.

Now we know what happened. This bitch had a baby by this dude around the corner from my house. They said they were from the west side and haven't been around there long. They said they were a robbing crew, who robbed drug dealers. They send that hoe to pretend she wanted to be with a nigger when she was really casing his place out. She worked out of the strip club, but she wasn't a stripper.

I told Drake what the streets were saying about that hoe.

He said, "I'll call you back because I just saw one of my partners with that bitch. Far them nigger concern, I handle that already."

I asked him what he meant.

He said, "Don't worry about that. My mom got some money that I promised to you. Go to her shop and pick it up."

I said thanks and hung up. I was at the store up the street from my house when I saw one of my godsons. I asked him what was going on. He said he was on his way to the hospital. I asked him who was sick. He said one of his friends, who just moved with him, around the corner, got shot six times.

I asked him if anyone else got hurt. He said there were kids in the house when they shot the house up, but no one else got hurt. They are scared, so now they are moving. I asked him what they do. He said that nigger probably ripped somebody off, knowing them. They were from that west side; you know how they roll. I asked him if they know who did it. He said my partner singing like a bird because he was scared they are coming back before they moved. His mom told him he better tell the police everything, and he did.

They had one of Drake's boys locked up for a drug charge, and he didn't have a bond. He called me and said that he just beat this bitch and broke her leg because he caught her stealing his dope.

I asked him, "What bitch.?"

He said, the one he grew up with and moved her in my room when I was moving out.

I said to myself, *I told that bitch I hope she gets everything she deserves and she is.*

He said, "It's a matter of time before that boy cut a deal."

I asked him, "Cut a deal about what?"

He said, "I need you to come and check out this new dope I got. They are saying something's wrong with the dope, and it's not coming back right." I said, "You my wife who went back up north? You know, she was one of the best cooks around." I told Drake I couldn't come. I told him, "I found out who set you up, but I think you already knew that." He didn't know I knew what he did, and I never saw him again.

My phone rang, and it was a collect call from Drake. I accepted the call, wondering what the hell he was doing locked up.

He said, "What's up?" sounding like Michael Jackson.

I said, "What the hell you doing locked up?"

He said, "One of my boys gave me up, and now they're talking about giving me thirty years."

I said, "Damn, you been to court yet?"

He said, "No, not yet."

I asked him where his bottom hoe at. He said his mother put them out and packed up all his stuff and put it in the new house he had bought before this happened; he was waiting to close on it. He said his mother closed on the house and moved out of the project.

Drake had to go, and so did I. A year had passed, and I was running my trap downtown, plus I was back running the hotel for the Hilda at night. My cousin called me, telling me about Drake. I told her that she was a dirty bitch for fucking Drake in my house while I was asleep. She kept saying how sorry she was for all the shit she had done to me. What she didn't know was I didn't trust that bitch far than I can see her. And payback is my reward.

I was leaving Stewart Avenue, and my cousin pulled up in the motel. I asked her what I could do to help.

She said, "This is my friend Gee Money." She got out of the car and said, "I just left the club, and Slim was up there."

Now she had my attention. She said he got a girl that work up there, but I heard he was on the run. They said they already locked up some of his family members.

She said, "You won't believe who Gee Money lives with and got a baby by."

I said, "Who?"

She said, "You remember that girl in school who you used to call your little sister? You and your girls used to leave school and go to her school when she said they tried to jump her because she was from a Dekalb County School, you remember?"

I said, "Where is she? I've been looking for my little sister."

My cousin said, "Gee Money sell weight, and I know you been looking for weight because one of the girls at the club told me you came up there but didn't want to see me. I been fucking with Gee Money, and sooner or later, I'm going to fuck the shit out of him."

I said, "I thought you just said you been fucking with him."

She said, "I'd been buying dope from him because he gives me extra. He always comes to the club when I call him. I'm going to fuck his ass because he's going to be mine."

And she said it like it was going to be true.

I said to myself, "Kingpin ha. Payback is always sweet."

When I got out of the shower, my phone rang, and it was Drake. I had been accepting his calls when he first got locked up. I haven't heard from him since.

He said, "Thanks for accepting my calls. They gave me thirty years because I took a jury trial like a dumb ass."

I told him how sorry I was for him and to pray about it.

Then he said, "I got married."

I didn't even remember hanging the phone up. I guess because I was laughing so damn hard.

Look for my next book, *Shot and Left for Dead.*

All true story by Miss Goldie, keeping it real.

About the Author

The author was born in Atlanta, Georgia. She has a husband, two daughters, three granddaughters, and a grandson. She and her husband runs a detail shop and tire and rim shop in Atlanta. The author was one of the first blacks to attend her elementary school, Meadowview Elementary in Dekalb, Georgia—she and her siblings. The author writes all her books with one hand because her other hand is partially paralyzed from a gunshot.

CPSIA information can be obtained
at www.ICGtesting.com
Printed in the USA
LVHW041159170520
655737LV00005B/553

9 781641 387453